Sleeping

Written by Josephine Selwyn

Picture Dictionary

bat

boy

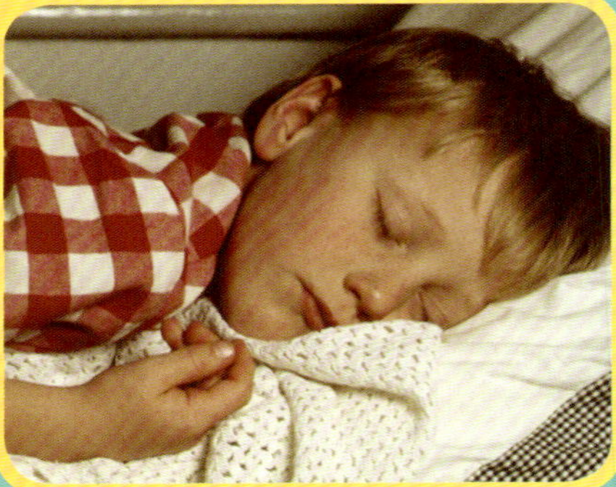

cat

Read the picture dictionary. You will find these words in the book.

dog

owl

pig

I sleep at night.

boy

I sleep in the day.

cat

I sleep at night.

pig

I sleep in the day.

owl

I sleep at night.

dog

I sleep in the day.